The Strangeness of the Good

JAMES MATTHEW WILSON

The
Strangeness
of the
Good

Including
Quarantine Notebook

 Angelico Press

For information, address:
Angelico Press
169 Monitor St.
Brooklyn, NY 11222
angelicopress.com

ISBN 978-1-62138-632-2 (pbk)
ISBN 978-1-62138-633-9 (cloth)

Cover Design: Michael Schrauzer

For Hilary

Companion through this strangest of years

But these Fuegians in the canoe were quite naked, and even one full-grown woman was absolutely so.... These poor wretches were stunted in their growth, their hideous faces bedaubed with white paint, their skins filthy and greasy, their hair entangled, their voices discordant, and their gestures violent. Viewing such men, one can hardly make oneself believe that they are fellow-creatures, and inhabitants of the same world.

—Charles Darwin

Now days are dragon-ridden, the nightmare
Rides upon sleep...

—W.B. Yeats

How can a heart given over to the affection of creatures be intimately united with God? I feel this is not possible.... It was not so for me, for I encountered only bitterness where stronger souls met with joy.

—Thérèse of Lisieux

CONTENTS

I

After the Ice Storm

The tree limbs cracked, the stopped car rocked,
   The village blacked out with the storm.
The shape of houses shuttered, locked,
   Weighed down the dark with darker form.

We looked up at the boughs, stripped bare
   Months ago with the season's turning,
But clawing now the anguished air
   To plead some hopeless case of yearning.

The wind whipped round us and our faces
   Burned with the dry burn of the ice,
In that most emptied out of places,
   Unmapped, unmeasured, shorn of price.

One night was all it took to give
   What men had built back to the earth,
Leaving it as no place to live
   Or contemplate a second birth.

We stood there, though, for what seemed long,
   The ice encasing everything.
We listened to wind void of song.
   We felt cold's unintended sting.

Those Days of Weighted Solitude

What one remembers is the autumn leaves,
The quiet avenues of Sunday morning
Weighed down beneath a quilt of rust and gold.
And, passing by the large, neglected houses,
Their porches slanting with locked bikes and couches
And occupants asleep still, having leased
Another hour till a headache stirred them,
One felt the world as still and damp and sad.
   Along these ways, I'd drag myself, head bowed,
The leaf bed softening my steps to silence,
But bowed as well beneath the gravity
My weekly pilgrimage had taken on:
To hear the back-door latch as it fell closed
Upon the darkness of the drowsing house,
And feel that solitude bear down on me
With absent weight, as I went off alone
To Mass. A few blocks down: the little church
With blunted turrets built of golden brick,
The shade of fallen leaves, and peaked with domes
Whose round tops balanced each a crucifix.
   I bore not just a sense of loneliness,
But sorrow and remorse, and would have gone
Alone, in any case, ashamed to share
With anyone this walk of half-belief;
This sense of contradicting not the world,
But rather all the world that dwelt within me.
   So also, in the inner chapel's darkness,
I'd sit alone, tucked in some pew's far corner,
Amid the surge of families crowded in,

Their hymnals clattering downward with a thump,
While some child, squirming at his father's shoulder,
Raised up at last a high and ceaseless wail.
I mouthed each prayer as if about to weep.
   I'd think of the apostles in their room,
Locked away with a wound of fear and failure.
And it would seem that I was there with them,
To pour out words at what had come to pass
In each of us. We did not understand,
But only could confess, the sense we bore.
   Then, heading back again, down that same path,
The Eucharist a dry taste in my mouth,
A sting upon my brain still heating me,
I'd wonder when this thing I had to do
Might seem less brittle. Would there come a time
I'd speak with golden tongue of all that glory?
Or, it not seem a glimmer swamped by darkness?
A time when every movement ceased to play
At parables about some inner mood?
   I did not know that there would be whole years,
Where neither grief nor joy could pound my chest,
And prayer came forth in one clean line of words
That carried nothing with it but its meaning;
The church itself seem bathed in neutral light,
My soul insensible in its detachment.
We do not always know when we've been blessed.

An Accident

The road flares burning where the truck swerved off
   Just before midnight show the streaks in gravel
And banged-up tailgate slanted in its trough.
   Those passing—weary, wondering—slow their travel
On sight of massed police and long enough
   To see provisioned brilliance unravel
In such vast darkness as to mask the face
   Of one who sobs in some unwonted place.

On the Water

The heron rises overhead,
   As we push off the reeded shore
   With our one cracked, muck-covered oar,
Across the pond's unstirring bed.

A bullfrog snaps within the weeds
   Just where, last summer, we found rotten
   Tackle, by fishermen forgotten
As they passed on to other needs.

I know, not far away, the world
   Despairs of rotten church and state
   And finds less cause for love than hate,
Its once brave flags now torn and furled.

I know as well, it was while hidden
   And thinking their room locked and bare
   The scared apostles felt flamed air
Send them to do as they were bidden.

The bright orange sides of koi slip by
   Obscured beneath the murky glass,
   And many darker things will pass
Before we hope of knowing why.

On Being Ill

Like death, which follows all, they grow more common,
The ill, gestating pain within their bodies,
Turned in upon it, marking down its savor
With such alacrity for shades of difference
That no one else can sense or listen to,
But merely watch as crooked fingers press,
Impatient, trying not to be unkind,
Until, at last, all trails off with a sound
Defying speech with its unfinished ending.

We see them tend each symptom like a world
Whose axis is pure pain; the library
Is full of invalids who scour pages
Of glossy magazines in search of remedies.
And others slump on stationary bikes
Down at the Y; tan, muscle-bound young men
Obliviously flex about them, while
Their hollowed eyes stare up at televisions,
Where smiling doctors chat of creams and diets.

The weight of weakness hangs from every hour
And all the future's qualified by phrases
Suggesting that, if it should really come,
It will be on the far side of a passage
Through a cold room, where one sits gowned in paper.
But then—strange thing—for those who do get better
(And almost all will, for a little while).
They leave behind not only all their studies
But even memory of what they've suffered.

Perhaps that's why Montaigne seems so unusual:
His willing resolution to turn inward
And notate with a delicate finesse
The disposition of each bodily organ,
And even the effects of fish or flesh,
The tour about his tongue of some old vintage,
Indifferent to the stone lodged in his groin,
Burning, its pressure building, unrelieved,
And unrelieving—ever—till the end.

The Children of Hamelin

Within the mountain that became their home,
  The children lifted up their cries in pleasure,
Their laughter bouncing, golden, free to roam
    From wall to wall, as they enjoyed each treasure;
    More was prepared for them than taste could measure,
      From candy floss to rocking horses, all
      Piled high about the glittering, echoing hall.

They dueled with wooden swords and painted shields;
  They dined on berries, cream, and golden cake,
While lounged on blankets they called battlefields,
    Unsure if they were dreaming or awake,
    But knowing every wish was theirs to take,
      And that the song descending with its trance
      Possessed their tired limbs and made them dance.

So great the harmony and clamorous din
  That filled up every moment of their day
And made the weeks, then seasons, seem to spin,
    They could not hear those noises far away,
    As their abandoned parents knelt to pray
      Then later, raised chapped fists up with a cry
      At the uncomprehending, empty sky.

The stony streets of Hamelin sank in quiet,
  The alleys emptied even of their rats,
Where once plump clerks and merchants had run riot
    With sales of wine and wares, fine gowns and hats
    To please the daughters of aristocrats.

Now only starving felines stretched in places
That once were filled with flushed and cunning faces.

The fountain's waters were shut off for good;
The old men disappeared behind stone walls;
While women, bent and sad, did what they could
By stationing the square and park with dolls
Whose arms forever spread to catch thrown balls,
Forever reached for some long-vanished treat,
Ears straining for the vanished sound of feet.

All Your Life

You'll earn less than you feel you're worth,
  Retire in debt;
Old faces framed above the hearth
  Your name forget.

And, friends forget your failings soon,
  But not your wife,
Who carries them like an old tune—
  Or sharpened knife.

You dreamed of politics and fame
  But that soon faded,
As no one liked you, though you claim
  You've just grown jaded.

You shuffle off to work each dawn,
  In every season;
What little good you've come upon
  Comes without reason.

Sameness and chance, catastrophe
  And empty hours
Will crowd out what you hoped would be
  Health, joy, and powers.

You'll read your children stories, teach
  Them how to pray;
But God and tale and all you preach
  They'll toss away.

Pythagoras had a golden thigh,
    The legends tell,
But yours of bone snapped with a sigh
    That night you fell.

And though the doctor says it'll mend
    With weeks in bed,
You've seen your whole life's downward trend
    Ends with you dead.

An After-Dinner Speech

Even now, we subject to mockery
  The old, officious, and avuncular
Postprandial toast; for, can we not all see
  Its mannered strains at dignity laid bare,
    Its emptiness encrusted in jeweled pomp?
    Such are the rites on which barbarians stomp.

He rises from the far head of the table,
  A snifter cradled near his vested paunch,
Cigar ash lengthening as he tells some fable
  From whose sententious finish he will launch
    On memories of an age consigned to dust
    And in whose morals we no longer trust.

But, he will carry on undaunted, he,
  Two nephews choking napkins in their lap,
A sister glaring in her cup of tea,
  And wondering where he's boiled up such pap,
    Of which it seems he has unending store,
    Even as his deafened aunt begins to snore.

We mock these things, though they've long passed away,
  And left no decent mores in their place,
And mock, though we have nothing else to say,
  No fine in-gathering rite or formal grace,
    But just an artery's solitary throb
    To stand unnumbered with the raging mob.

Revolutions

The world's so cruel now, they say,
 Demanding revolution;
That someone be strung up or shot
 Is the preferred solution.

The broken backs of myriads
 Have paved roads for the great;
So, topple statues of the dead
 To swat the hand of fate.

The books shelved in the library
 Lead us ourselves to spurn;
So leave them in the rain to rot
 And all their words unlearn.

When paradise does not arrive
 Despite bone piled on bone
The revolution turns at last
 But to devour its own.

It comes as well for those who plead
 For thought and beauty's case,
Their high-walled pleasure garden flattened
 By blunt boot and smug face.

But, nonetheless, those who would make
 Or savor some good thing
Must carry on as if at leisure
 Although the dark hoards ring.

Babushkas

The Polish girls in Cicero
  Pinched their babushka knots,
As the cold wind blew through
  Brick alleys and bare lots.

They pinched them tighter still
  When boys came whistling by
And kept their faces lowered
  To sign what they'd deny.

The walkup stairs would creak
  As they returned at dusk
To pad the chops in flour
  And part corn from its husk.

They'll dream of Canfield's soda
  While sitting in the night,
A needle pushed, then rising,
  To darn their torn socks tight.

I know such days are over,
  Where manners spoke unsaid,
And want, pain, fear, deep longing
  Worked themselves out in thread.

But they're the lasting figures
  My mother's memory taught
For all such silent passions
  That can—if just—be wrought.

Through the Water

*he must in some way cross or dive under the
water, which is the most ancient symbol of
the barrier between two worlds*
                    —*Yvor Winters*

Far back within the mansion of our thought
  We glimpse a lintel with a door that's shut,
And through which all our lives would seem to lead
  Though we feel powerless to say toward what.
It is the place where all the shapes we know
  Give way to whispers and a gnawing gut.

And so, in childhood, we will duck beneath
  The waterfall into a hidden cove;
In summer, pass within a stand of pines
  Cut off from those bright fields in which we rove,
Whose needles lay a softening bed of silence
  And great boughs tightly weave a sacred grove.

When winter settles in, and our skies darken,
  We take a trampled path by pond and wood,
And find beneath an arch of slumbering thorn
  Stray tufts of fur, a skull stripped of its hood,
Then turn and look down through the thickening ice
  In wonder at the strangeness of the good.

And Peter, Peter, falling through that plane,
  Where he had only cast his nets before,
And where Behemoth stalked in darkest depths
  That sank and sank as if there were no floor,

He cried out to the wind and felt a hand
    That clutched and bore his burden back to shore.

We know that we must fall into such waters,
    Must lose ourselves within their breathless power,
Until we are raised up, hair drenched, eyes stinging,
    By one who says to us that, from this hour,
We have passed through, were dead but have returned,
    And are a new creation come to flower.

From the Dream Journals of Denis Devlin

10 June 1932

I'm in a cinema. The darkness smells,
But all around, fresh-faced Americans
Light up with me to hear the chorus bells,
See bride kiss bridegroom, as the camera pans
Away from them and up into the sky,
Until the village church and grey-streaked cloud
Disintegrate in celluloid and die
To purest white like Christ's flash-printed shroud.

I slap my hands down on the rests to rise,
And think the audience should leave—we all
Should leave. But, then, I notice one girl's eyes
Are still fixed toward the stage. She starts to call,
And so does everyone, but I can't hear.
All silence, and the screen a brilliant white,
As squads of stiff-necked Free State soldiers steer
A woman and a child before our sight.

They seem a small black mass, a huddled blot,
Beneath the towering blankness of the screen.
And I am seized with fear; the crowd grows fraught
Just as the pair morphs to an antique scene.
"Ah, yes, it is the Blessed Virgin, yes,"
I say, and watch her cradle our small Lord;
Then think, "Who are they trying to impress
With this cheap advertisement?," and feel whored.

We should take issue with the management.
It's bad enough with soldiers in the streets
Shooting the cornice to their hearts' content;
They shouldn't stoop to fatten their receipts.
But it's too late. The figures disappear.
And now the screen fills with a young girl's face,
Her tearing eye and curl of bloodied ear,
The jaw, a liminal and blurring trace.

Vita Activa

The engineer, grown loose with his third drink,
   At last confesses he can't bear to sit
   Quiet, but must be digging in his pit,
Mind pressured by some task at hand to think.
And so, his friend, the teacher at a school,
   Agrees: his satisfaction, toiling hours
   With children, testing out their nascent powers,
Where each thing taught becomes a useful tool.

Who doesn't love growth, gain, initiation,
   To find the boy without a place his niche?
But, in the raising of some tower of glass,
   The figure solved, the player's perfect pitch,
Fulfillment lies beyond the act: to pass
A moment, paused in silent admiration.

The Thought of God

What, with your being so absolute and full,
   A beauty without limit and a love
That needs no object—like a seated bull
    In shade, that neither man nor fly can move—
     Don't you get lonely?
Our fathers thought it was implausible
   That you be anything but thought itself,
Innascibile and incognosible,
    Far out of reach, perched on some starry shelf,
     You and you only;

Which struck me as unlikely, who'd incline,
   If strong enough, to trample Hector down,
Then glory, one boot pressed on broken chine,
    And with a glare send packing every clown
     Who challenged me.
It's not the cunning (ring clutched in their paw
   And counting on invisibility)
Who seem as gods, but those whose faces draw
    All eyes to them, whose great virility
     Will let none be.

The adolescent thinks how Zeus came forth
   In feathered raiment, fell in golden shower,
Or, with Europa riding, plowed the swarth;
    His lust would mount each comely form with power
     To serve his joy.
That's what our instinct thinks it knows of gods;
   It chafes at every hint of idle boredom;

Prefers to go to war or play the odds;
    It's heard the prophet's voice, but then ignored him,
        Whose words annoy.

And, when we do not hear your voice in turn,
    We think we have been set free from a coward,
Too alien to make a young heart yearn,
    If good some time ago, a good long soured,
        Whose headstone crumbles.
Or, is our answer in your darkest silence?
    So near to us it throbs beneath each nerve,
And with its stillness cancels out our violence,
    Waiting within the time that you conserve,
        Till our thought stumbles.

"Every Morning He Hallowed Himself"

While still a student, wandering abroad,
   But lodged in Dublin for a long July,
   I'd pass, each day, through King Street with a sigh,
Dismissing all I couldn't afford as fraud.
I'd reach the busy end of Grafton Street
   And join its host of tourists on their way
Beneath the Fusilier's arch, in fanned retreat
   Into the Green beyond, and there delay
     Before bronze statues set along the path
     To figure those who'd felt the empire's wrath.

My daily route would bridge the small lake's heart
   And come out just beside the bust of Joyce,
   Where we would listen to that clamorous voice
Which formed a sentence from each place and part:
The vulgar, hocking wares; the verdant growth
   Surrounding those immortalized in loss
And who spoke only through a diecast oath
   That made on history's text a marginal gloss;
     The narrow gate, where branching birch and lime
     Gave shade like Marvell's garden out of time.

And then, before the stoop-browed church of brick
   That Newman built, scrunched in between a pair
   Of Georgian homes, I'd silence thought for prayer
And leave behind the mind's desultory tick:
Stray images from Mahon, lines from Yeats,
   Some thought of Maritain's I couldn't decide
The sense of—these were left with other freights
   (The future's dark, or past wounds to my pride),

As if they dropped within the postbox there,
Before I'd mount the lion-sentried stair.

Once in the college's marmoreal cool,
  I'd take the narrow staircase at the rear,
  Where Hopkins muttered once in self-sunk drear,
Where Joyce had tramped with martyr, crank, and fool;
And Newman raised his cassock round the knee
  To climb, as I did, marking each flight's turn
With prayer before each statue that he'd see—
  The mind's lit incense pausing there to burn,
  For, Joseph, Mary, and, at last, the Lord—
  That soul and body rise with one accord.

How callow it must seem, that first attempt
  To measure out my days as if they were
  Some liturgy whose borrowed form might moor
A life adrift, misshapen, and unkempt.
We pass so absently from phase to phase—
  I know—that conscious disciplines seem vain;
But even now it sets my heart ablaze
  To see that young man bow to foreign reign.
  With him, I, older and unruly still,
  Would have my will reordered by His will.

II

Good Friday, 2013. Driving Northward

Traveling once, early, through rough country sunk in its own
    darkness,
The car's nose snuffling blindly for a path, my stupid promise
To be at home before the children woke somehow obtaining,

I lifted up my eyes and saw, above the weighty masses
Of Appalachian slopes, the sky withdraw from their deep
    blackness,
The slumbering stillness peaceably resuming its old shape.

Things drew themselves together, not by any knife's clean
    paring,
Or like the long ink line across an upper-third of foolscap,
By which the artist of a sketch anoints a new horizon.

It was, instead, like to deep breathing underneath a blanket,
Where things declare themselves by being what they are
    within;
So much, it seems, that every blessed thing which comes to
    light

Stands forth to show its birth from that first fruitful wakeful-
    ness
Who wakens us by some abscondant gleaming in the eye
For nothing but to see that all is blessing, all is light.

The Teachers

A father's rough hands, hung with fingers laced,
    Are all the eye may ever learn of prayer;
The young ear in the settling dark feels graced
    To hear those notes a mother's lips can spare.
And every wildness of our fallen state
    Comes crying through the child wrenched from sleep,
Such wounds as by long discipline abate
    And leave the old man's silence calm and deep.

Even the flit of time instructs the mind
    As it bears in and out each tempered tone—
The brightening early shoot, the ripened rind—
    Before wind-scoured ice can raise its moan.
These figures can so make the conscience ring
    That speech, which follows, seems a poor, dumb thing.

My Grandmother's Kitchen

Christmases, my grandmother set
  A crystal tray of cookies out.
She'd claim they were homemade; but bet
Against such folksy verity,
  For emptied cartons lay about
The kitchen where we all could see.

Could see, that is, had we just cracked
  The heavy portal to that room
Which guarded stove and icebox, lacked
Nothing her husband could afford,
  But seemed a cell of heat and gloom
Where chops thawed on the cutting board.

It was her inmost privacy
  Around which all that house would turn,
And from which good things came to be,
By what brow-glistening toil, what pride,
  What fussy cunning, none dared learn
But, with our hunger, stayed outside.

Inhabitants

I know. You've spent this whole day wandering
   Through clumps of trees and seen the sunlight shine
Until that gushy heart is all a-swing
   At God's deft needlework, so soft and fine.

Yea, like some vicar mounting to his nest,
   You sigh and stutter sweet and gentle words
That all is love, but we are loved the best
   (A bit more even than those charming birds!).

But man's hands spoil everything they touch;
   And someone following after you will spoil
The scene with shifty eyes and thieving clutch
   And make you weep we're sprung from common soil.

Then, you will preach a different sort of text,
   Just like the naturalist who turned explorer:
Each painted face he saw left him perplexed,
   And made him feel our brotherhood with horror.

Premises

She's just an awkward girl, her face too small,
Who owns a pet shop; he, dark haired and tall,
Unemployed, but still more than she could wish—
Until, one night, he stops to buy a fish.
Fled from Los Angeles, from debt and drugs,
The bearded actor feels three gentle tugs
Upon his pants. Is it an orphan boy
In need of help and friendship—or a ploy?
He cannot trust, been hurt too much before.
A kid with no legs kicks the winning score.
You wake in pain, wrists bound and eyes swollen shut,
And hear the click-clack of the whore's heeled strut.
His rented flat was sloppy, face unshaven,
At night he'd drink and talk to his pet raven;
The neighbors think him lonely, sweet, and say
As much, when man and bird are hauled away.
A singer with a past. Old women driving.
A traveling salesman caught for too much wiving.
"The night was cold, my husband three months dead,
A song he'd sing kept cycling through my head,
As if it held some last request in riddle."
Scene One: an old share cropper strums his fiddle.
Christopher Kingston had it all, both wife
And wealth, but something soon would *change his life*
Forever: a brown package in the mails
Containing (camera peeks) clock, charge, and nails.
Six brothers come to mourn their widowed father.

A snake escapes the zoo, but they don't bother
To search for it till kids start going missing.
"The walls were thin; we heard the codger's hissing."
A stolen car, some cigarettes. A monkey
Made out of gold? Two cats swiped by one's flunky?
An East Berliner born with lobster hands.
Swiss terrorists who issue strange demands.
The county fair where someone mean gets his.
The Jewish boy who wins a TV quiz.
The one in which a cruise ship starts to burn,
Parting two newlyweds, but teaching stern
Old Simkins that "the story of his years
Was not quite done—and will leave you in tears."

The Failings of a Master

And then he turned and seemed like one of those
Who race across the fields to win the green
Cloth at Verona; and of those runners, he
Appeared to be the winner, not the loser.
                              —Dante, *Inferno* XV

A note received from an old friend concludes
   He's looking back on all his work and finds
   It poor, as if the meeting of two minds
Rebuked the young and spoiled the old man's moods.
Things that were born of hopeful quietudes
   And came out with a blazing light that blinds
   Seem now a crude machine of squeaks and grinds:
Triumphs the retrospective eye denudes.

Humility sustains the living saint;
   Sweet Francis called himself the worst of sinners.
And so I take these words from such a friend,
But make them judge of mine without constraint,
   To see his least performance lap my winners,
Then disappear around the road's far bend.

Halfser Astray

Young Halfser's laundry hung from every shelf,
His sodden sleeves and slacks on stretched display.
He'd done his washing in the sink himself
And hung them thus, who knew no other way.

He stared through a wet armpit out onto
The sidewalk east of Stephen's Green, whose shoe
Soles' clack against the stone reminded him
Of free days out beyond this sodden scrim.

The sun dissolved, a tab of orange detergent.
He waited, waited, held off his emergent
Hunger to ramble as the Dubliners do,
To drink their stout and gorge on their lamb stew.

In all his dreams of tramping through the world,
He saw himself posed in cafes with books,
Or on the Seine or Rhine's bank, white sleeves curled
About some girl with Continental looks.

The sour notes his Brooklyn accent mucked
With foreign air, came out like dry champagne,
And dry his wit, and, yes, the shirttail tucked
Into his waist stayed dry in Paris rain.

But Celtic twilight is no good for laundering,
And so, in squishy socks, he set out maundering,
The sound beneath his feet much like that sound
A man hears, lost at sea, and knows he's drowned.

A Rocking Chair Song

You know, my son, that I'm no griper,
But this is your third soiled diaper
   Tonight; the third I've had to bag
   And run outside before I gag.
I hear, in darkness, the pied piper.

But what I do not hear is quiet;
Your sweet voice, risen to a riot
   At one and three and five each morning,
   As soft as a tornado warning;
If sleep came for a price, I'd buy it.

And, while it is some consolation
To rock you through that cry's cessation,
   Just as I feel your body ease,
   It arches for a mighty sneeze
That sprays me with a strange potation.

The joys of fatherhood are great,
Not least to lull your gentle weight
   Within the cradle of my arms;
   And great, the floods and the alarms,
Which come so frequently and late.

The Reluctant Scholar

Sit down, my child, to your thick books.
Enough with all those dirty looks,
But turn to page one-hundred-ten
Where Daniel's in the lions' den;
And then, to chapter fifty-eight,
Where you'll learn how to calculate
Beyond the limit of your fingers
At whose stub tips the novice lingers.
We'll finish off our morning course
With Greeks hid in their wooden horse.
Those warriors had been lost and blind
Without Ulysses' myriad mind;
And Daniel felt the lion's tooth
Had faithful thoughts not set him loose;
And if you will live in this world
Where mysteries wait to be unfurled
As clues to God's divinity,
You'll have to cross infinity.

But, Mother, I've been turning pages
For far too long; it seems like ages
Since I did anything but read.
There's other things that children need.
We must go hunt stones in a brook,
Not to count out, but just to look
Upon their slick and mottled shades.
At noon, the enemy invades
(I'm sorry it puts you out of humor;
My scouts confirm the awful rumor),
And I have yet to make my maps,

Prepare the troops and set the traps,
Arm all my friends with shields and sticks
To give those beastly Greeks their licks.
Studying all day is such a bore.
Please, let me up and out the door.

What's this complaining all about?
The Greeks unloosed their awful shout
And made a ruin of old Troy
Though it was no great cause of joy.
At dawn, the king came, his head hung,
Thinking Daniel no more among
The living, but soon found him there
Because he'd memorized his prayer.
Whether you witness cities smolder
Or warn them, as a sage grown older,
Numbers will stay with you, and counting
Is one path for the mind's sure mounting
From mystery to mystery;
For minds can think what eyes can't see.
Arithmetic's a sign of that.
But very well. Stop where you're at,
Your pile of books has had its say,
Go chase those sneaking Greeks away,
Escape some lions, find some stones,
And quit your count of schoolhouse groans.

Golden Age

Though Ovid measured
With precious metals
And Auden treasured
Lime, for it settles,

I'd say that ages
And men will all
Slip through such gauges
Material.

But rather, young
Men think their names
Will soon be sung
As deathless fames

Of noble beings.
While men grown older
Know that most things
Grow weak not bolder,

Then lie, and molder.

At Middle Age

Upon this anniversary's ledge
    I see the years ahead,
Obscured by nonexistence still,
    Are fewer than those fled,

And, with the waking of this day,
    Comes news Tim Murphy's died,
His body worn away by drink,
    But mind sure in its pride.

Even at ten, I stood in dread
    Of how the hours passed
And looked at every season's turn
    With longing it would last.

What sorrow came with summer twilight,
    As the mosquitos neared,
And voices called us from our play
    Until the yards had cleared.

What certitude, though, Murphy had
    In his returning home
To those wide flats of prairie grass,
    The adding poem to poem.

Little less sure have I been of
    What I've received and made;
The home we've built, the children raised,
    How little their price paid.

But that just coldly clarifies,
    Whatever we may say
Of living well and making rich,
    Small epics of our day,

That calculus of time's firm passage,
    Relentless, without rite,
Alone is cause of fear and circled
    By ever-encroaching night.

A Common Tongue

My family's was a plain, laconic speech,
    The sort intended never to impress
But, with a grudge at broken silence, reach
    Its point and stop, if it could do no less.
Small wonder, then, that all extravagance
    Should once have struck me with a blush of shame
And yet still drew my eyes as radiance
    Wielded a power I sensed but could not name.

But wonderful indeed that, having known
    Deep labyrinths and the colosseum of stars,
And even claimed their glory for my own,
    I feel at last how gaudy excess mars
A line, and find a measured dignity
    In that rude speech that was first given to me.

First Day of School
After Christmas

The frosted grass winks light
    And crunches underfoot,
As day reclaims from night
    The shade of leaf and root
And lends it to our sight.

We cross the backyard's plain,
    You and I off together,
As we did in fall rain
    And in the warmer weather,
And as we shall again.

I steam the air with words
    That fathers tell their daughters,
Taking the part of birds
    Who've fled to lapping waters
Or lands of grazing herds.

But you say little back,
    Will sometimes smile, if just;
The grind beneath our track
    Of winter's crystal crust
Attends the speech we lack.

A father dreads that space,
　　Wherein comes awkward silence,
Where what was set in place
　　Seems jostled by some violence
And strips the dawn of grace.

And yet, we still walk through
　　This chill that blankets all.
For, what else could we do,
　　But hear late blue jays call
And watch the day renew?

Imitation

Not long ago, it seemed the fashion
   To preach that man was born alone
   And died that way, in somber tone,
As if no one could know one's passion.

Yes, dreary in our solitude,
   We sit propped on our wooden chair
   Our thought, our anguish, every care
Trapped at an airless altitude.

But was it ever so, this posing?
   The infant in his mother's lap
   Already imitates her tap
Of heart, her self himself composing.

And all our thoughts are woven from
   Threads bare with crossing times before.
   We tread upon an earthen floor
Mounded by prints already come.

And though shales piled as a cairn
   May seem locked in their loneliness,
   Aspens too stiff and mute to bless
The neighboring boughs for which they yearn,

Their roots are tangled in the deep,
   Their weight is pressing all to one;
   And that is less than we have done
Who, at another's pain, will weep.

This Marvelous Being

How long it lasts, his gazing in the glass,
   Before his parents stir behind their door,
Before he hears the furnace light its gas
   And warm the tile of the bathroom floor,
He cannot say, so rapt is he to see
   The darkening hairs that shade above his lip,
   To comb them back with thumb and finger tip
And marvel at becoming come to be.

Not far away, a father fills his mug
   And lifts the blind to show the black outside.
The day's beginning he greets with a shrug,
   Suspending every thought he must decide,
And turns to fetch the milk. There, on the fridge,
   Cling faces of his children in cheap frames,
   And now he lingers, murmuring their names,
As one stares out in awe from some high bridge.

III

QUARANTINE NOTEBOOK

A pure thing, against the sad affairs of earth
> —Czeslaw Milosz

joyfulness is given as a quality grounded in the sight
of the sky
> —Dietrich von Hildebrand

*Tout est à moi, catolique, et je ne suis privé d'aucun de
vous. La mort au lieu de vous obscurcir
Vous dégage comme une planète qui commence son éter-
nelle orbite,
Parcourant des aires égales en des temps égaux,
Selon l'ellipse dont le soleil que nous voyons reporte un
seul des foyers.*
> —Paul Claudel

March 15, 2020

The great tree in the neighbors' yard has bloomed;
White blossoms hang like egg shells in the air,
While down the road the restaurants shut their doors.
The rising noise, the swish and fade to silence,
Of traffic by our home grows less and less.
The schools have closed and all the nearby houses
Sit stout and quiet, ready to erupt.
But, while some stores stay open, I take off
To find my season's load of hardwood mulch
To blanket black the dormant garden beds.
A friend of ours was in Milan last week.
His father died. He'd gone to bury him.
The last flight out of there was his. He's back,
But shut in solitude for fourteen days,
His wife and children's voices calling through
The flimsy barrier of the bedroom door.
He must still hear the grief of Lombardy,
An echo of the heavy bell against
The stone of narrow streets too late deserted,
The guarded stillness of the Duomo square.
Our shops are being ransacked, shelves stripped bare,
Even the fruits and vegetables are gone.
And all because of some sharp woman's panic
(Her years of playing activist on Facebook,
With all those postured sentiments, give way
To hoarding claws and serious, darting eyes),
The cunning of some man who sees his love
Ends quite precisely where the fence line runs.
But I return home with the car's rear end
Weighed low with seven musky bags, and toss
Them one by one like limp, resistless bodies

49

Along the walk. I take up rake and shovel,
Begin the small, familiar, yearly tasks
That after a long winter one must do
To overcome its slow decay, to greet
Old life's new start, and ready all the house
For what may come that we cannot yet know.

March 17, 2020

We hear from news reports the young are out
Crowding the beaches, getting drunk as usual.
The brilliant images of sea and sand,
Which under normal circumstances draw
The mind to thoughts of pleasures so removed
From life they seem a floating of pure body,
Now crackle with invisible contagion.
   A boy whose cheek bones are burned lobster red,
His eyes crazed with the margaritas sipped
Since dawn, brags loudly for the camera
He's going to get his money's worth or die.
   I go to tour the decimated stores,
To find, among picked-over wares, some leavings,
And cart them home for breakfast. But I go
Mostly to marvel at the emptiness,
To see myself what mania's wages look like.
The clerks already have things half restocked.
   It is Saint Patrick's Day. My wife has found
Enough corned beef and cabbage and potatoes
To feed the seven of us, evening come.
   When the kids woke this morning, Ceci crept
Downstairs and found the living room a mess;
A chair lay tipped; a shoe hung from a lamp;
Yesterday's paper lay in wrinkled sections
And mingled with a rift of stickered school work.
But there, amidst it all, beneath the couch,
She found the little green box she had made
To trap a leprechaun. Yes, he'd been here.
It worked. He left a pot of golden candies,
His messy tricks the price we pay for magic.
Well after dinner, when the plates are stacked,

A smear of mashed potatoes and thin ribbons
Of beef all that is left, so have we feasted,
I scrub the kitchen, sipping pints of stout.
	Then, Ceci asks to watch *The Quiet Man*.
I've told her that a leprechaun is in it,
Which, should you see small Flynn, his pointed ears
And plotting smile champing on his pipe,
You'd know is true enough, although it's not.
The kids love every minute. From his bed,
I hear James humming out its bouncy theme.
	Some young man on the news sings his odd tune,
Later that night. He's cleared out all the stores
For three states of their cleaning wipes and Lysol,
Their rubber gloves and soaps and who-knows-what,
All which he'd planned to sell online for gold.
He almost brags about it and I wonder
How long it might take till he meets his fate
In some strange accident that no one sees,
Save for a darting swirl of faerie lights
That rise on air and vanish in the gloom.
	And in the days that follow, Ceci wakes
Before us all and sneaks downstairs in search
Of candy in her trap. She wants him back,
Her leprechaun, and cries to find him silent.
	Then, tricks begin to overtake the house:
My dresser drawers left open like a staircase;
A glass of milk hid in a closet; toys
That had been put away clumped on the rug.
"The leprechaun is tricking you," she says,
To have his golden presence back by cunning
Though it's denied by time's too punctual magic.

March 22, 2020

The deaths are mounting, far across the water.
And here, the sages of the internet
Equate this hour with the rule of Stalin,
As, first, New York, then California, call
For each to make a gulag of his room.
The rumors say that martial law is coming.
   But we sleep late. There is no Mass today.
The pastor of St. Monica's says his,
On our behalf, within a cage of silence.
   When all the kids are at the breakfast table,
Their cereal bowls cleaned, save a splash of milk,
A sodden flake or two that drape the side,
I pull my missal out to read the Mass.
   "You see and hear this all your life," I say.
"This morning, we'll go slow, so you can learn
What each part's called. You know that Jesus is
The Word of God, and so, at first, we hear
That Word, receive it by our ear through scripture.
But in the second part, we do not listen;
No, we receive the Word upon our tongue."
   Thomas's fingers fiddle with his puzzle,
A map of the United States, and flip
Out Arkansas upon the floor, while Livia
Keeps eying *manga* girls that she's been drawing,
Which, lithe in fashion gowns, sport doctors' masks.
   "This morning we will hear the Word of God,"
I say, "but cannot eat it." And we do.
We read of Jesus bending to the ground,
And mixing dirt with spit into a clay
To heal the man who has been blind from birth.
When that's all done, the Pharisees complain.

And both the blind man and his parents cower,
Afraid the miracle might break the Sabbath,
Until dismissed and sent back to their home.
    We finish, and I think of that old painting
O'Kelly did, a Connemara Mass
Said in a thatch-roofed cottage, where the priest
Is making final blessing over the heads
Of those who crowd in prayer on soiled knees.
A woman bends still lower, to the dirt,
As if she's desperate with some cry for mercy.
Two altar candles shed a holy glow
On this great mystery performed in secret.
    Later that day, while strolling past the table,
Meaning to put a pot of coffee on,
I see that Livia has gowned her figures
In dark and heavy cloaks and sketched in plague masks,
With bent proboscis, rounded, blackened eyes,
And, rising from one stiff-clawed leather glove,
A long staff aimed to point out where we suffer.

March 25, 2020

I thought that looking back upon this time,
I'd view it as the winter without snow.
Out for a walk the other day, I heard
The steady roar of a snowblower running,
Its owner burning off the tank of gas
He'd filled, in late November, when a trace
Of flurries made its feigning fall toward earth.
We do not always read the hour rightly;
The signs the times bear with them are obscured
As if by gusting snow squalls in the headlights.
   And now, it's something else that falls. The virus
Is spreading through New York. A friend of mine,
Holed up in his apartment in Manhattan,
Sends photos out of cans of beans and franks,
Beef chili, paired with bottles of cheap wine
And *Gawain* in a tattered paperback,
All captioned with quotations from Defoe
And laughter at the way he's been marooned.
   A decade back, I recollect, we shared
Bottles of Yellow Tail at a reception,
And talked of Auden late into the night.
We met the morning after, our heads pounding,
Just like Sir Gawain, knelt in winter snow,
Who waited for the Green Knight's falling axe
That, with one swoop, both spared and chastened him.
   The fearful flee that city like a flood;
The wealthy spilling out into the Hamptons,
Where all the year-round residents, who pour
The drinks and scoop the ice cream through the summer,
Are saying, now, don't come, we cannot take you.
They've covered up the welcome signs, would raise

The bridges if they could, the hospitals
All full, the groceries emptied, far as Montauk.
   I was supposed to catch a New York train
Today myself, but that, of course, is cancelled.
And so, I sat, this morning, on the couch
And read my boys the opening of *Five
Children and It*. Dear Panther and her siblings
Have fled the pestilential streets of London,
Where things are labeled with invisible signs—
Keep Out, or *Do Not Touch*, or *Go Away*—
And every bit of fun gets one in trouble.
They find themselves left at a country house,
Much like the Hamptons, if not quite so nice,
Its chief appeal a neighboring gravel pit.
   While digging to Australia, one day,
Their errant spade turns up a Psammead,
Who startles with his gruff voice, snail-like eyes,
And furry little body snug in sand.
They little know that he will grant them wishes:
Such useless guineas men stare at like sores,
Or giant wings with which to beat the air
And rob a farmer's plum trees of their fruit,
As if avenging angels sent by God.
   James blasts his trumpet in the living room;
The straining pip-pip-pip of reveille
Flies unobstructed through my office door.
It is—oh, yes—Annunciation Day.
How little we expect the news we hear,
Until it comes upon us, brilliant, blazing,
Commanding we not feel the fear we feel,
And that we must unlearn all that we know,
So as to see the hour with new eyes,
And, what is more, to trust, somehow, we will
Endure that fate whose stroke has yet to fall.

56

April 1, 2020

For Hilary

The rising light of early morning falls
On kitchen table, tucked-in chairs, and finds
At last the open floor's dark-paneled wood.
There, fifteen months old now, John Cassian stands,
Smiling and naked, save his new-changed diaper.
He takes three gambling steps before the fridge,
Then lowers down, in fear of his own powers.
      This walking is all new to him. I think
That he is of you and you're here with me,
Though also upstairs, catching one last hour
Of sleep within the heavy-curtained dark.
That is one gift for you, that final hour,
To start our fourteenth anniversary.
      My brother's called to say he's got the virus:
Electric cables jolting through his blood,
And fever sweat anoints him with its crown.
He lies in bed and thinks of the Pacific,
Two miles away, as if it were the start
Of boundless freedom and of paradise.
      When we hang up, I scan the morning paper,
And find each headline bellows out its number:
The count of dying, dead, or newly ill,
Of unemployed who wait for promised checks,
Or homeless in Las Vegas left to squat
In painted hopscotch squares upon a tarmac,
Until the shelter can reopen. What
Of this will we discuss at morning coffee?
What will we do behind our bolted doors
To mark the depth to which this day transformed us?

The children watched Duck Soup the other night,
The hundredth time or so we've put it on.
What starts in pageant and diplomacy
Soon veers, with Harpo's motor bike, to chaos,
Descends by an incessant squeak of horns,
And, through a trial as fake as those in *Lear*,
Lands, sprawling, finally, on a battle field.

And there, within a humbled, bombed-out shack,
Groucho's long, wayward quest for Margaret Dumont
Reaches some kind of end, in such a place,
Where fate not only brings two loves together
But guarantees that Groucho can't escape.

How grateful he must be for tanks and shells
To keep them both holed up. Even though his mouth
May rat-tat like a wild Tommy gun,
Undoing pleas of love with sudden wise cracks,
There is no getting out of her great arms.
Am I, like him, a sharp-tongued unromantic?
Or do you see, behind the fake mustache
And lit cigar, eyes roll with adoration?

The hour doesn't lend itself to slapstick.
One friend, with his black sense of humor, notes
That if the virus doesn't get us, well,
The Yellowstone volcano probably will,
Or more tornados charging up from Jonesboro,
And, failing that, an asteroid is due
To brush by earth, the final days of April.
He doesn't plan to stick around to see it.

Under the circumstance, it's no surprise
The news reports a case of tragic love.
A husband and his wife, afraid to die,
Hide in their home and watch the President,
On television, mumbling on like Chico
About the promises of chloroquine.

They find some on the shelf, or something like it,
And though it's labeled, "Poison: Don't Ingest,"
They mix it with their Pepsi. In an hour,
The husband's dead, the wife in hospital.
The darkness would snuff out our morning light.

A friend in Colorado also writes me,
Explaining his long silence with a story.
A month ago, his wife ran off the road,
And could remember nothing of it, after.
Her back now broken, staring at the lights
Above her bed, she listens as the doctors
Inform her husband that her neck and brain
Are riddled with small cancerous growths. And now,
The hospital sealed off with quarantine,
Her husband drives her there each week, then waits.
She disappears within. An hour goes by.
The doctors fight her death in short, quick bursts;
And then, she's pushed back out and they drive home,
Her body drifting with the car through daylight.

What does her husband feel, again beside her?
One more punctilious duty in a life
They've shared and go on sharing as they may?
The rhythm of their marriage troubled, yes,
But carrying on, one treatment at a time?

Or is it something more? This friend of mine,
Who's always had a streak of Groucho in him
To meet the darkness with a snappy word,
Does he now feel the oceanic weight
Of love? The kind that lifts you up and pulls
You out, and drags you deep into the tide,
And says, from now on, think of nothing else
But that you cannot bear to lose this one
You love. Feel your ambitions drop away,
Your defects and your failings, too, and give

The little that is left to try to save her,
And hope for nothing but that she will live.
    I stand here in the kitchen, where I started,
Shaken by what comes calling from afar,
The halting, stumbling steps of doubtful futures,
And think, there is no gift that's adequate
To greet you at your waking, on this day.

April 5, 2020

We wait and wonder how this all will end.
When can we go to Michigan?, the children
Keep asking, unaware and filled with hope,
While everyone else tries to understand
What it might mean that things are getting worse.
   Our village flushes, bloomed with daffodils
Whose bulbs lay deep, forgotten through the winter,
Only to push up now in early spring.
They tell us with their mellow prettiness
Nothing that we have eyes to understand.
   Most of us look instead for news, or turn
To aging books whose pages leave a dust
Upon the fingers as they're read once more,
As if to say that nothing lasts forever,
And even books will taste oblivion.
   In one, I happen on an arcane wonder,
A man half brilliant and half charlatan.
The Jesuit, Athanasius Kircher, fled
To Avignon, Vienna, finally Rome,
As thirty years of war ignited city,
And court, and Church, and left the age exhausted.
But he, the while, towed about with him
His cabinet of curiosities;
Within its dark, he kept the last stray knick-knacks
The learning of the Renaissance had gathered.
He'd show them off to courtiers just come
Back from the siege, their legs and fingers shattered,
And faces blistered red with powder burns.
   "The world is bound with secret knots," he wrote,
And claimed to have untied a few in books,
Decoding hieroglyphics, speculating

That in the depths below Vesuvius,
An ocean lay, whose forces rule our tides.
For, are not all appearances effects
Of things invisible that we detect
Chiefly within the eyeless dark of reason?
   His mind was grand with theories that were wrong:
Some just bizarre, but others plump with insight,
Because he trusted that the world could be
Read by the one who hoarded up its items
And ordered them as in a lexicon.
   So, with his blurry microscope, he showed
The blood from victims of the plague played host
To swarming armies so minute they seemed
To promise every war-wrecked world concealed
World within world, and each one's rage and strife
Begot the blasting sickness of the larger.
   We see on TV, Governor Cuomo speak.
Seated behind a table, answering questions
The camera cut in just too late to catch,
He says things never will return to normal.
There is no going back for such a people,
Grown crazed with boredom, locked in their apartments,
And staring down on ghostly avenues
To watch the ambulances racing past.
The flashing lights and sirens fill the void
For one great, crashing minute, while inside
A gasping body, eyes alit with terror,
Joins those whose names we will not know, but who
Will soon be counted with the mounting dead.
   A friend of mine, who studies economics,
Says she's with him: says all she sees beyond
These weeks of idleness is loss on loss,
The banks and factories, the gaudy wealth
She used to warn against as our day's idol—

Or totem, really, warping our desires.
All this, it seems to her, will not come back.
And though she's often wished some modesty
Might be restored to us, this vanishing
She does not welcome, knowing how the young
Will soon be left to stare, expectant, out
On debt, dashed plans, and permanent decline.

    I don't pretend to see into such darkness
Myself. I've watched the alcoholic ruined,
Then wakened to a new day with his vow
To free himself, and make his earnest try,
Only to fall back in familiar habits.

    I think as well of those who suffered Dresden
Or Dachau, how they must have thought the waste
Spread all before them was the final vision,
Beyond which lay the leveled, worse unknown.
And yet, they, even in their resignation,
Felt, against all desire, seeds of hope
And made, within that speechless sorrow, sketches
For how a new world would be built on ashes.

    Customs may not be good, but they are dogged;
And hope is not a choice, but what we do,
When our mind stretches out to feel the darkness,
So long, at least, as we can still say "worse."

    Kircher's contemporary, Blaise Pascal,
The mathematician and apologist,
Wrote that our hope was still another trace,
A mark made in the wreckage of our souls,
To tell us we are not born for this world,
But for another that we lost and seek.

    On every side, infinities surround us,
And all our partial reasonings can manage
Is to cast out our thoughts like poker chips,
Small bets we place on hunched uncertainties,

63

A gesture pointing toward a great abyss
That won't unveil itself until it does.

   Just think of those, two thousand years ago,
Who veiled the highway to Jerusalem
With palms, as Christ rode in. They felt they knew
Just what he was, and bid their flashy welcome.

   And think of those who stared up at him hanging,
Then turned to find their homes through early darkness
And took their dinners at an empty table.

   And think of those who felt the early spring
Run through them with the chill of day's first dawning,
Which seemed so bracing in its emptiness,
So stripped, so opened by the cleansing light.
They stood amid the quiet of the garden,
And waited, for the first time, without hope.

April 8, 2020

The vodka bottle, blue as buried sapphire,
Has lain near empty on its side, a year
Or more, forgotten at the freezer's back,
Beneath the bags of strawberries, fries, and nuggets,
And thickening with a glaze of permafrost.
    The state stores being closed, and suddenly
Without the means of buying more, I dig
It out. This is no era for martinis,
All briny and medicinal, but sweetness,
Compensatory, generous, and concealing;
And so, I watch it flow like syrup, down
Into the crevices of ice, then top
The highball off with juice. This hour of night,
In normal times, I'd take my drink and sit,
A book in hand, to catch the baseball game.
    I'd alternate between the back-and-forth
Of lines of verse that volley down the page,
And glances up to see the Cubbies' struggles.
There, on the screen, encircled by the crowd
(Who turn their backs upon the world, and yet
Provide a noisy solitude), the pitcher
Shakes off a signal, nods, winds up, and throws.
    At such remove does art find concentration:
The thing made stiffens toward integrity,
Nine doubtful innings fumble to a whole,
And thus take on a kind of permanence.
    The season, like the liquor stores, suspended,
I feel myself fall back on younger ways;
I'd sit up reading till the early morning,
A sleepless, lonesome undergraduate,
And switch, as hours passed and I grew weary,

From book to book, with each one lighter, easier,
In sequence, till my eyes at last dropped shut.
    As I did then, I find myself once more:
Alone, a crop of titles at my side.
I open up Milosz. It's like a phone book,
And not more interesting, at first, it seems:
The listing, hazy images of dreams
Mistaken by their source for prophecy.
    But, when the Nazi tanks roll into Warsaw,
The spine at once grows straight, the ruined street
And what lies buried in its sudden wreckage
Become too serious and lost for playing.
A pile of books, stacked in a roofless building;
The lambent face of Giordano Bruno
Surrounded by the busy market stalls,
The chatter as the tourists spoon gelato;
The poet staring on his father reading,
On broken statues, churches, emptied ghettos.
His voice cries out in heavy lamentation,
To see the art that he had meant for freedom—
A flight of butterflies, a taste of vodka
Burning, then disappearing, on the tongue—
Must come to something far more serious.
His natural love would have preferred affairs
With all the European capitals,
To savor brilliance without consequence
And traipse from place to place and settle nowhere.
    But now, he's rudely forced to take dictation,
To make a record of what's been destroyed,
Preserving too in ink the names of those
Who laughed, so pleased, to be the ones destroying.
He's had to root his love and hatred down
In one foundation lest it be forgotten,
Resigned himself to play the mournful witness

Who digs in deeper as he heads to exile.
   The minutes creeping on toward somnolence,
I pull out my collected Betjeman.
His boisterous, thumping ballads make me think
Of Kipling, or what Eliot said of him:
It may not come to poetry, but verse
Contains its own perfections and, he adds
(Perhaps a little envious), it's verse
That people memorize and say and sing.
They'll clap to lines on Exeter and Croydon
While sighing above their pints, and with a curse,
Summon the friendly bombs to fall on Slough.
To which there's no replying, but with "cheers."
   It's such an easy, accidental contrast.
The serious poet, witness, visionary,
As formless as a ghost, but weighed with lead,
In confrontation, first, with Nazi troops,
And later, with a whole regime of lies,
As Russians came to be a second master;
And Betjeman, who failed at math, but could
Stomp out a rhythm with his drunken hoof
To set the patrons rocking on their stools
And let them know their island's not so bad.
   But I'm not done. I find upon my stack
The Story of a Soul. And there she is,
Thérèse, that round face floating in her habit,
Who tells us not all flowers can be roses,
That we must take such grace as we are given.
   I'm not the first to see her infant freedom,
That liveliness which tumbles into trouble
And teeters high upon a kitchen chair,
That flighty glee to play at kings and queens,
Will carry her just where she's meant to go.
All freedom seeks its fullness in a cloister;

All laughter merges with the prayer of Carmel;
In solitude we find our company,
And speak most frankly in a form commanded.
   So much we can discern within that portrait
Of her dressed up to play Saint Joan of Arc,
That wild mane, parted, draped behind her armor.
One hand upholds the flag of *fleur de lis,*
The other lightly rests upon a sword.
How freely she would give herself away,
To burn within the fire of Christ's love.
   O, lady of Lisieux, I think, you found
The form where depths reveal their splendid glory;
You are the living image of perfection.
But then, the mind adrift, the hour late,
I think as well how perfect form appears
Within the pitcher working from the stretch.
His spine upright, his rear foot on the rubber,
His eyes indifferent to the facing batter,
And conscious of the runner just behind him,
He holds his glove raised up to hide his face.
And, in the leather darkness of its womb,
Mysterious and patient, he will form
An arc of flight to catch the outside corner—
Chosen for just this moment and that man,
But also in response to what has come
Before, and what will follow down the count.
Each pitch contains, within its narrow compass,
The splendid, sprawling thoughts of past and future,
And yet remains a thing of concentration,
Whose name proclaims itself in what it does.

April 15, 2020

The children whirl in circles round me there,
Axis and father of them all, their bikes
Humming against cold air, the flash of wheels
Ripping about the empty parking lot
Outside the shuttered public library.
   The only person who intrudes upon
Their endless, free procession: one old man
Who comes each day and plugs his laptop in
With an extension cord, its long orange line
Led snake-like to an outlet in the stone.
He sits there, in his car's back seat, a door
Cracked to admit the power, his white head
Ignoring us and bent in concentration,
As if pure thought turned in upon itself.
   But he should see how those kids whip their way
In narrow, then in greater, orbits flying,
As do the hosts of feathered seraphim,
Formed rank on rank, enclosed in brilliant wings,
And giving of the plenitude they circle,
From greater to the lesser, so that all
Share in the splendor of the sourceless font,
That boundless wheel of light which kindles all.
Such ecstasy and glory have they found
In their but recently acquired balance;
They coast within a haze of radiance.
   Beyond us, stretch the baseball fields, their backstops
Heavy and dull with chain-linked uselessness,
The diamonds scribbled through with dirt bike tracks.
And, just along the margin of the wood,
The playground we have named for Narnia
Sits idle, swings and jungle gym both wrapped

In orange police tape, snapping back and forth,
Caught in the fitful gusts of April wind.
    Just out of sight, still other circles narrow.
The nesting of a man into his lounger,
A case of Lite spread open like a mouth
Beside the leg rest handle. On the set,
An episode recorded some years back
Shows someone spin the wheel or shout out "O."
    A woman, frail and shrunken in her blouse,
Has freshened up her tight perm with a pick,
But let it drop back gently on the couch,
Her breath grown shallow, slowed as sleep descends.
And, in the early morning, fathers pace
With bloodshot, angry eyes, the children yelling
And crowding one another at the sink.
The basin's thick with aqua streaks of paste
That cling beneath the cold gush jetting downward.
    And somewhere, someone's mother chips a nail
Trying to clean the juice and crumbs that hide
Within the wrinkled padding of a highchair;
And someone locked inside a studio
Whose heart is racing, racing with the boredom
Reels eyes from phone to book to alley window;
While in the paper, blotches pullulate
And overlap upon a printed map
Like an old stack of tiddlywinks we've scattered.
    Our dogwoods now stand prim with pinkish flowers,
The maple in the side yard, bulging clusters,
While apple and magnolia shed last petals
In skirts that radiate about their trunks.
    Yet, even now, the season's gripped with chill,
And I find, twisting on the air, a few
Stray flurries wend their pointless journey down,
As if to warn us, all that comes to pass

Will be turned back upon itself, in time,
However much time seems one long, straight line.
And, in this spiraling about an axis,
We may see fate, but fate has its own order;
And order brings with it a kind of freedom,
As Thomas proves, when he repeats each arc
About the lot, as if it were the cosmos—
That place of churning planets, winding stars,
And singing angels covering their eyes—
His cycle racing wild its spinning pageant
So fast I hardly note the trepidations.

April 18, 2020

Our James has on his secret service suit,
Black with black tie, and little dangly ear piece;
He strolls around the house, as if at ease,
Then suddenly, unprompted, pulls his gun
And sends a Nerf dart shooting through the air.
He's got good aim. He's tagged me in the throat
Before, and more than once has stung my ear lobe
While my back's turned, and set me crying out,
"What did I do?" as if there were an answer.
    We catch the footage coming out of Lansing;
The honking train of cars that fill the streets,
And spread out—sort of—people with their signs,
Protesting quarantine. But what exactly?
Notices posted in the stores declare
A ban on sales of garden tools and seed,
Which seems a bleak and ominous restraint.
The ghost of Roscoe Filburn stirs the darkness
Of his Ohio boneyard, and heads north
To seek revenge at last, his spirit planting
Itself in all those souls with flags and Trump signs.
    How vile indeed it seems to tell a people
It may not grow its food and feed itself.
Perhaps, however, they are just afraid
That liquor will be banned and breweries fail,
Or looking for excuse to get outside.
    The president chimes in on cue, of course,
Endorsing all the clamor. Then the press,
Hearing the bell he wears around his neck,
Summoning them to dinner, pass their day
Debating and attacking all his words.
My Lord, it's like they cannot stop themselves.

And he, up at the rostrum every day,
Reciting unrehearsed but scripted comments
In such a soporific drone, we think,
His mind is elsewhere, limbering for the spat
Set to ensue the moment he extends
A finger, puckers up that face, and tilts
His head, to take the first outrageous question.
  Why is it that he says the things he does?
The theories range from rank malevolence
To just a wicked, prankish sense of humor.
Whatever else, it's certain he takes pleasure
In sparring with that den of those who hate him,
And every thought that passes through his mind
Will do the trick as well as any other,
To hold out, wriggling, for their eyes, like meat.
  The other night, I took a call from students.
They'd read *The Waste Land* as a group and wanted
To learn exactly what it meant. It seemed
A pile of foreign lines and gibberish
To them, though here and there, as with the stones
Handsel and Gretel scattered in the woods,
They sensed a pale white gleaming in the moonlight
As if some inner brilliance were drawn out
And almost made a path for them to follow.
How strange, that father in the fairy tale;
That he should leave his children to the forest,
And then return home, sulking in his tears.
  Why is it that we do the things we do?
Why write a poem whose lines are blasted trenches?
We find it as disordered as the market,
In Wuhan, where the fish are stacked on ice
And stare with lidless eyes at dangling meat hooks
From which chops dangle as if brushing shoulders;
Where plastic tubs overflow with chicken livers,

And grey bins hold small crabs that stretch their claws.
   Desires, Thomas Hobbes writes, are but motions,
Secreted, writhing rhythms in the heart
That work their way out from our inner meat,
As does a splinter, till it shows itself.
   The misery of humankind is rooted
In this. Our appetites are all obscured,
Don't tell themselves behind our poker faces,
Until we act—and then, it is too late.
The boy has ripped the dolly from his sister;
The mugger's got a knife against your throat;
The army has already laid its siege
About the city, with its cannons aimed
Upon the store house, where, it cannot know,
The sacks of wheat already have run low.
   A person's not a mystery, just opaque.
To see into our hearts is little different
Than breaking rock. We open up the darkness
And find inside the belly of the stone,
More stone, identical, and dull, and cold.
   That's what Hobbes tells us, anyway. And seeing
Our public spectacles, one may incline
To grant the point, to boil all things down
To stimuli and reflexes, as if
Psychology and billiard balls both ran
On the same mechanistic principles.
   Just like the virus then, and we begin
To wonder where it started. Did it hatch
In some bright Wuhan lab, where all was clean
And clear and rational, and not the least
Bit interesting to us, until it sprang
Its foul parasite upon the world?
Some fellow pedals on his bicycle,
A sack of groceries dangling from the bars;

Some woman shakes the carpet from her stoop,
And stays to watch the dust descend on puddles
Left over from a night of sickly rain.
Some boy, a clutch of marbles in his fist,
And looking for the sun through morning mist,
Between half-finished buildings on his street,
Sees how the idle crane still bears its load,
A slanted girder drifting in the air;
He pauses, shuts both teary eyes, and coughs.

April 22, 2020

 The dome of clouds above us rests in silence,
And silent rest the roads and parking lots,
The surging rush of motors gone, surrendering
The emptiness to one low, constant growl
Of wind that roves about like dogs turned feral.
 You join them, those who linger in the dim
Gray atmosphere and stand in tape-marked squares,
With coats and gloves, and masks upon the face.
You wait to be admitted to the store.
The eyes, retired and blank, look toward the clerk
Whose handset crackles with the next directive.
The skin grows moist with breath beneath its wrappings.
 And, once inside, you fill your cart with milk
And bread, and follow arrows on the floor,
To trudge the narrow aisles, back and forth.
A gray-haired woman and her escort brush
Against you and it's instinct to recoil,
To stare at one another half a moment,
Uncomprehending, not sure what to do,
Your voices muffled and expressions masked.
You think, what are they carrying within?
You think, contamination's on my sleeve.
And then think, how ridiculous we are,
And turn off, down the aisle with the tea cakes.
 Years ago, we already felt this loss
Of trust that leaves one staring at one's neighbor
As either an indifference or a threat.
And that was when we still could see their faces;
Now, we're like Cheshire cats, but in reverse,
Our thoughts concealed by disappearing mouths.
 Each night, a janitor from Chester rides

Two buses and a train on his commute.
Within the crush of fellow passengers,
He keeps a tube of sanitizer propped
Upon his lap, as if a talisman,
And runs an antiseptic wipe across
The seat, each time the person next to him
Descends into the blind of city lights.
And then, at dawn, he does it all again,
On edge and waiting to get home and shower.
   I've heard some people speak of empathy
As if it were the sterling of all virtues,
And talk of reading novels as a way
To build compassion, make the brutal kind,
Forgiving what we cannot understand,
As if the act of dramatizing pain
Were one with our desire to lessen it.
A taste for literature can soften hearts,
Such persons sometimes say, before they cast
Their eyes with cold disgust on anyone
Who does not share their generous convictions.
   I thought of this the other night, while reading
Some pages from a book by Matthew Arnold.
He claims indeed that culture raises up
The soul above its petty class and interests,
Refines it of cliché and prejudice,
Enlightens it to see the truth of things,
And draws it from the mire toward perfection.
   He argues this with such exasperation
At those buffoons who will not hear his meaning,
Those philistines who snarl from crabbed kirk pulpits;
Barbarians who recline with drowsy eyelids
In mannered silence through his speech, and offer
A brief, indifferent, "Quite," before they turn
To tap a spoon against their hardboiled egg.

He must have felt his lambchop-whiskered jaw
Wear out, at last, sweet eloquence with rage,
To see his reason's light leave all unmoved.
Barbarians will remain barbarians still,
And philistines still fumble with their hymn book,
While counting out their profits from the mill.
    Perhaps, a gospel of mere empathy
Is not the panacea for divisions
That fester in the street or voting booth,
But run right through the shivered heart of man.
Perhaps, it's not the only sort we need.
    While sitting just this morning over eggs
And bacon, with the kids, I read aloud
The eight beatitudes. In fact, I read
Them twice, because they're hard to understand;
Because as well, being middle aged, I know
They don't exactly stick within the memory.
So, "Blessed are the clean of heart," I said,
"For they shall see their God." I was so moved.
"Compare our hearts as to the bathroom mirror,
Smudged up with fingerprints and splattered toothpaste.
The clean heart is the mirror that is wiped,
A mirror that reflects the face of God."
    And Ceci looked at me and tugged my hand.
"Do you remember what the Queen of Hearts,
In *Alice*, says?" she asked. And I had not
Yet seen within her heart how she'd misheard,
Before she rose with pomp upon her chair,
Her plastic spoon an all-commanding scepter
To summon shuffling soldiers to her deck.
"Off with her head!" she cried, and cried again,
"Off with her head!" And we looked up at her,
Her eyes as bright as mirrors in the sun.

April 30, 2020

    Last weekend, summer came to California,
So, all the cooped-up, sheltering-in-place
And withering-to-paleness citizens
Invaded beaches up and down the coast.
A girl in her bikini ran through spray,
Its iridescence veiling soft, lithe legs
That stretched and leapt above the silvered sand—
Her hair slicked back and trailing in dark cords,
Her body given to the wind's caress.
News cameras beamed her form around the world
To show us freedom is voluptuous.
(This morning, though, she's locked indoors again.)
    We saw her, briefly, on TV, before
The winds here, raging through our towering oaks
And sloshing maples like drenched, heavy mopheads,
Knocked down a powerline and cut her out.
I look up at the clouds, their ominous convoy
That blots out all the sky, and know the world
Is angry and has other plans for us,
Though like a houseless Lear, I may not name them.
    Cecilia overheard some other news.
A company has turned our firemen,
Our doctors, cops, and nurses into dolls—
Or, anyway, that's how the broadcast phrased it.
She sees them staring right out from the screen,
Those plastic eyes and smiles fixed for good.
"How did they turn them into that?" she asked.
    "Magic," I said, and magic I say now,
Writing this in the glare of glowering sky.
    But Thomas steps right in. "There's no such thing,"
He says, with all the urgency of one

For whom the question's very much alive.
  "I'm sorry," I reply, "then how would *you*
Explain how people were transformed to dolls?"
It's as I thought: he has no better theory.
But his round, freckled face is firmly set,
The dimples deepening with doubting dogma,
And stubborn for a fact he thinks he knows.
  Just yesterday, I had a conversation
About the place of meaning in a book.
Not *what* the meaning was, but where it is.
The young man I was talking with insisted,
A bit like Thomas, that it's in our heads,
Not in the book at all. He mentioned Gödel
And after that I couldn't really follow;
It seemed so much a thick and shaggy nonsense.
  We raised the question of the waterfall.
The same old problem Kant and Goethe mulled,
When men still looked with patience at the world
And saw its urgent metamorphoses,
And wondered was it stranger or a friend,
A womb of symbols or a canvas for them.
"The waterfall is beautiful," we say,
But are we speaking of the waterfall,
Or what the waterfall has made us feel?
Such nonsense, as the young will sometimes speak
To make themselves feel hardened into age.
  But, I stare up at clouds like great gray hosts,
Abroad to conquer everything they see.
I hear the wind set strong, broad shoulders low
And ram against our helpless house's side,
And do not speak, but wait within its powers.
  I wait, and live again in thought just how,
The other day, I bent with naked chest
And leaned my lowered head above the sink.

80

My wife stood over, with a pair of clippers.
She touched the shagging gray about my sides,
The stiff hairs curling over ear and nape,
And razed them—slowly, patiently; her hand
Gentle and firm to keep the head in place—
That locus given too much weight by others,
But humble and receptive to her palm.
  And down and down into the silver drain,
The dull hairs sheered in squads of iron tuft,
And lay, absorbing droplets from the nozzle,
Until my crown was light and clear again,
And I rose up, that my still-lively face
Might turn receptive eyes once more upon
The gowned and gleaming symbols of the world.

May 1, 2020

On Saturdays, I go to help with Mass,
To lector and recite the intercessions.
On Sundays, in the kitchen, all the children
Will watch the video broadcast of me there,
Which plays, while I fry pancakes on the griddle.
You wonder why one curious miracle
In many of the saints' lives is the act
Of bilocation (Why, of all things, that?),
Until a day like this when it is mimicked.
And then, you realize that we all want
To be both fully present in the flesh
And yet give *some* clue that our spirits can
Stretch out beyond themselves, can penetrate
The lives of others in a real communion.
      We see it in those lots overgrown with weeds,
Ringed by a span of rusted cyclone fencing,
That not so long ago were drive-in theaters.
They are once more. Their hulking, weathered screens
Kindled with light, the cars drawn slowly in,
Their tires following half-hidden ruts,
The long grass stroking their warm underbellies,
Until each comes to rest and windows lower,
The inward darkness opened to night air.
And now, all stare, perhaps alone together,
Or, maybe, joined, their interwoven gaze
Converging on the smirk of Jimmy Stewart
As only celluloid can bring him to us.
      Our souls indeed slip freely through the world
And touch on everything with their attentions,
As nothing that has being is a stranger,
But rather gives itself to sense or mind.

So, Livia, when we take our walks together,
Wrenches the stroller from my grip and runs,
Her body almost floating down that sweep
Of hillside road unwinding like a ribbon,
Her legs a flash of energy and spirit
That sprint as swiftly back to where I follow.
I catch the baby cheering out his "wee,"
Which floats right up to me upon the wind.
It was supposed to be track season, now,
And I, supposed to watch her from the stands;
But this is better for us both, I think.

   What we most often call the need for freedom,
To manifest one's self without constraint,
Is rather this, it seems; the need to enter
By means of our ungated, bashful spirits
Into some kind of commerce or communion.
We share by nature in the life of things,
And meet the world as face encounters face.

   But, how that need, misunderstood, miscarries.
The tour guide in Antalya, freed from lockdown,
Who scaled a cliff to view the Düden Falls,
And stretched out from the ledge to snap a picture
For sending to her mother and her friends.
She clicked, her smile haloed by the mist
That rose from plunging torrents toward the sun.
A family saw her, out, beyond the guardrails.

   The crash of water being what it is,
It took three days to find her body, where
It lay, indifferent, pinned against the rocks.

   Now, May Day comes, memorial of the march
And bomb that shook the market in Chicago,
Where uniformed police and strikers met.
It takes its place in every calendar,
As if all union were by force and violence,

Achieved against the grain of our own growth,
And fated for our sad commemoration.
   We do so poorly what is natural
That we suspect that nature is a liar;
Feel rattled by such names as love and justice;
Fear we shall be destroyed by what we need;
We, who know well we're called to be together.

May 9, 2020

    The spade, fetched off its nail within the shed,
Swings with a heft beside me as I go
To pay the garden bed out back a visit.
The frosts have passed. The time has come for planting.
Grey, hardened clods slice cleanly off the blade.
Dead leaves that cluster in the rough, and stems
From pepper plants pulled out and left to dry
With last November's swift and hardening freeze,
Go down into the darkness, while the earth
Gets raised and turned to show its loamy black.
    I glide the spade to level out the soil,
Then point its edge and tally rows of troughs.
These guide my work: to sift each pepper seed,
Minute and ivory, off the palm and down,
Then tamp the soft dirt over, gently patting
Just as you might a dog's deep flank of scruff.
    And now, I pull a sleeve from my back pocket.
The air is cool, the sky a marbled brightness,
The kind that makes you raise your head in hope.
And so, I tear the paper seam, and tap
A chunky clutch of mammoth sunflower seeds
Into my palm. Then, stretched on hands and knees,
I drill a row of deep holes with my finger,
And nest each seed beneath a layer of soil.
They'll measure out the season with their growth
Until the children can return to school.
    I know that, far from here, the farmers run
Their tractors into fields grown ripe with beans,
With glabrous, greeny heads of cabbages,
And plow what they've raised back into the soil.
Onions lie piled in newly opened trenches,

The backhoe sifting dirt on their white skins.
And others steer their pregnant dairy trucks
Right to the edge of stinking compost pits
And flush a thousand gallons of fresh milk.
No one to pick it all, no one to buy it,
So back and back into the ground it goes;
The fields of Florida and Idaho,
Great wastes of idle, rotting fruitfulness
On which their stewards stare at loss for speech.

How much is being buried now, that stood,
Just days ago, among us, full of life.
I hear from friends up north, the *Boston Globe*
Runs on for pages with obituaries,
And watched, last night, in silence, as my wife
Sat on the couch and spread the local broadsheet.
Her fingers traced a bow beneath the lamplight
With such a dancing, tranquil elegance
That suddenly stopped short to find them there,
Lined up in columns running on for miles:
The grainy, ink-stamped faces of the dead.

I hear, as well, a story from Virginia.
A friend of ours, expecting her first child,
Has gone out walking in the countryside,
The red clay faintly glowing in the fields
Beneath alfalfa, tall pines arched above.
She stops to pick some clover, while a woman
Glides past her on the narrow walk and smiles.

She sits down in the long and shaded grass
That lines the trail, then smooths her dress, and spreads,
Upon the shrinking parcel of her lap,
The little bunch of clover that she's gathered,
To note the variegations on the leaves.

But then, she senses someone standing by;
The woman who had passed has now returned.

I don't know why it was she thought to do so—
Made curious, maybe, by such idle study.
But, seeing the little pile of trefoil leaves,
And, seeing the rounded fullness of her dress,
The woman says, "It looks like you're expecting."
There, in the pleasant silence that descends,
She raises up a flattened palm and prays,
Our friend's eyes softly closed and her head bowed
To take whatever blessing here was given.
   Oh, let them grow, these flowers of the sun,
And let those buried crops beget anew;
And let what has been lost not be forgotten;
And let the world know seasons once again,
Where we can stare in joy unmixed with grief
On all that grows and spreads upon the earth.

May 14, 2020

My brother calls, the virus long since passed,
And he back at his desk, as if it never
Had knocked him out or shaken him within.
"Do you just write about whatever happens
Around your house or in the yard?" he asks.
  "I worked my shed into a poem last week,"
I say, "So, yeah, I guess." Outside my window,
The songbirds raise a fugue of rapid twitters,
And crows erupt with loud, shrill interjections.
  But, deeper, on the lower frequencies,
I hear the hum of digger and of crane,
A couple blocks away, their steady signal
That, all at once, construction has resumed.
The houses left unfinished, their garages
Like gaping mouths that bare the plywood darkness,
And lumber stacked before them like a tongue,
To these the crews return and take up hammers.
  This working up quotidian life to poems
Just seems absurd to him, who for his living
Will turn a dollar into something useful,
Produce a thing that someone else will buy.
His way of life depends upon his seeing
How value can be skimmed from what was worthless,
Or, from crude stuff, some good that others want.
Just writing down what was already there
Does not seem right.
                Of course, that misses what
Is actually occurring, when one takes
The settled details of the ordinary
And sets them rhyming one against the other.
Or, when one takes the plain prose of the hour,

The news report, the anecdote, the thought
That passes through the mind while one's out walking,
The odd thing that one's daughter said at breakfast,
And straitens it until it fits in meter
And runs in coded columns down the page.
It's no less striking than what came of Daphne,
Her body hardened into ancient wood,
Or to those sisters who took up their perch
Within the mazed coiffure made of her boughs
To sing each other's sorrows in the dusk.
Like other business, this not only finds,
But enters in, refines, and raises up
Until we see the mystery that was there
Persisting, yet transformed, as something new.

  Von Hildebrand writes somewhere, what we call
"Prosaic" is man's taking of the normal
And ruining it by mere routine, until
It seems mechanical or bureaucratic.
The adze the carpenter runs down a plank
Transformed to whirring blades and smoking engines;
The great bazaar, where carpets hang for sale,
Reduced to rented office suites whose clerks
Sit sighing with their fingers bent on keys.
We know just what he meant. As Percy said,
The whole world sometimes seems deep-sunk in sameness,
In sameness carries on, of sameness dies.
We yearn to be shocked out of what may kill us.

  But Livia claimed this morning that I've said
Otherwise: art affirms the ordinary.
And, yes, I probably have. For, do we not
Turn back upon what's plain and most familiar,
Such things as we know well yet do not see,
And suddenly discover what they are?

  So, Plato noticed that, because we think,

And thinking is an immaterial act,
We must have souls; and, since our souls cause motion,
They are its origin and, thus, immortal.
But he's not through. If our souls are immortal,
They must in their vast motions have seen all,
Including that great pageant of the gods,
Who circle far above us, savoring beauty
As it shines forth from that which truly is,
The whole world ordered by their whirling thought.
   Just staring inward on those things we know,
Our vision passes through and lights upon
What we would never otherwise have guessed.
And that is just what happens when our prose
Is sounded for its measured syllables
And forms itself to numbers we call verse.
   Some doubt that it is possible to find
A god concealed within a homely man
Inclined to argue with himself in doorways,
Or that those seated at a dinner table
Could learn within the breaking of their bread
All that there is to know of truth or grace.
And so, they go in search of strange sensations,
They check the headlines for celebrities
Who've been tattooed, divorced, or wound up dead
With some mysterious substance in the stomach.
The virus numbers growing stale, they read
About a slaughter in a hospital,
And tally up the children carted out,
Or watch in wonder—once, and then again—
A man get shot and crumple on the pavement.
Still anxious for some change, they even dream
Of death as a disease that will be cured
By some new gadget we can wear, or pill
That hasn't been invented yet, but will.

But, turn away from this. Yes, turn away.
Our immortality is here, already.
It comes in even through the open window
That brings the rhythms of the daily round;
That looks down on the children in the yard,
And sees their play with sticks and grass and toys
Build new worlds at the center of the old;
And lets us lift our vision far beyond,
To find, between the oaks grown still at last,
The centering spire of St. Monica's,
Which draws the eye up to its ringing height,
Which stands impassive to the fearful hour,
And lends the side arm of its iron cross
As eyrie to a preening red-tailed hawk.

Epilogue, May 17, 2020

    My wife and I stopped, half a block away.
We stared up wondering what it was we saw,
That form alighted on the church's cross.
    Two months ago, I idled in the yard,
The spring just threatening to persist in cold,
And leaned upon my spade's smooth, wooden handle,
Dark masses stretched before me on the ground.
    Forever, in a book, Achilles stands
Among the ships that plough the shores of Troy,
Howling in anger at fierce Agamemnon,
For claiming her who is his rightful prize.
Meanwhile, around them, plague pelts down like rain.
    Not far away, a couple is descending
The shaded trail that follows Ridley Creek.
They stop before a massive fallen trunk,
Which vaults the water like an ancient bridge.
Its sides are caked with moss; its root bowl spreads
Its splinters in a ruined crown; its length
Is bleached and rotted at the top from sunlight.
They climb and take it to the other shore,
Where all gives way to trackless wilderness.
    And here, where shadows run from noontime light,
Three robins hop and pick about the grass
To feed on insects burrowed in the soil.
    Our public life has been so far debased
That all we've left are mobs of partisans
Who shout suspicions of conspiracies
Across the clashing waters that divide them.
For, only secret plotting could explain
The sickness, tyranny, or idiocy
That runs through everything and topples all.

In this, at least, the public's like the private,
Indeed, is one with it. The neighbors grousing
At kids who ride too close upon their bikes,
With face masks dangling; every moment, now,
Lies tense with shadows like the leaves of grass
Through which the robins dart their yellow beaks.
    That is why Thales of Miletus cried,
All things are full of gods. We cannot help
But feel their meddling whims just out of sight,
That all appearances are by design,
As when a stagehand, couched behind the backcloth,
In momentary carelessness, will fumble
And drop a saber waiting for Act Two.
It shatters our absorption in the scene;
Or, rather, make us conscious of its form—
The accidental item, turn of phrase,
Or motion pitched above us in the sky,
All suddenly revealed as well-made pieces
Within a world that's cracked, yet full and deep,
And trying to tell us what to think of it.
    It's been my pleasure to record such things,
My occupation, too, and honest study;
My wish: to open wide the welded doors
Of minutes, and to draw the mortal hours,
With their uncanny oddities and flukes,
Together as some whole—provisional,
No doubt, but also, in its vexing way,
Enduring. This I offer as a gift,
For it was always yours as much as mine;
What tracings I have made here with my hand
Are yours to look within, their deeps to sound,
To figure how the whole thing fits together.
    I only ask, you keep in mind that plots
May be malevolent, but most are not

And show themselves as sturdy in the end
To those who bring attention and good will.
   Be as I was, when I was still a boy,
And turned up early at my grandma's lake house.
She'd taped a note in blue ink on the door,
That squarish, trembling cursive of her hand,
To let me know she'd gone out to the store,
But left the door unlocked. I was to enter
The shady porch and make myself at home;
To wait within the quiet and the stillness;
And pass the time by eying all its clutter—
The Corky skis, the lures, rods, and nets—
Those things acquired in a life of summers,
And kept not for their owner but her guests.

IV

When

When noisome crowds turn out to flood the beach,
   And with their flesh despoil all in reach;
When some boy burns his hand and squeals with pain
   Only to touch it to the stove again;
When, waiting for a carousel at the park,
   You see pale, tattooed bodies purpled dark;
When this drunk stranger brags with all his force
   About his past adulteries and divorce;
Will you look on it all, just as you should,
   And, in that sordid wreckage find the good?

When you turn over leaves upon the vine,
   Where lantern flies cling, gorging each veined line;
When great winds shake the trees and cut the power,
   Leaving you in the darkness of the hour;
When, in the nursing home, your mother dies
   Cut off from muttered prayers and useless cries;
When every argument begets a roar,
   And every careless thought erupts in war;
Will you maintain what once was understood,
   That, even now, the world as such is good?

And when they hunt him through the soaking heat,
   To leave him crumpled on a bloody street;
And when, behind calm eyes, he seems to gloat,
   And press his weight down on another's throat;

And when you see them standing calmly there,
    Indifferent as his last word dies in air;
And when the glass is cracked, the streets aflame,
    With no words spoken but that burning name;
Will you stand as the Lord of All once stood,
    And somehow say that things are very good?

Acknowledgments

Versions of all these poems first appeared or are forthcoming in various journals and magazines:

"After the Ice Storm," "Those Days of Weighted Solitude," "A Common Tongue," and "Quarantine Notebook," in *Dappled Things* ("Quarantine Notebook" was published online in full, and excerpted and republished in the print magazine).

"An Accident," in *First Things*; "On the Water," "My Grandmother's Kitchen," "A Rocking Chair Song," and "Imitation," in *National Review*; "On Being Ill," in *The New Criterion*; "All Your Life" and "Every Morning He Hallowed Himself," in *North American Anglican Review* (subsequently anthologized in *The Slumbering Host*, eds. Clinton Collister and Daniel Rattelle); "An After-Dinner Speech," "The Reluctant Scholar," and "Golden Age," in *Forma*; "Revolutions" and "Babushkas," in *The Agonist*; "Through the Water," "The Thought of God," and "The Teachers," in *Unleash the Gospel*; "From the Dream Journals of Denis Devlin" and "This Marvelous Being," in *Literary Matters*; "*Vita Activa*," in *Evangelization and Culture*; "Good Friday, 2013. Driving Northward" and "The Failings of a Master," in *Chronicles*; "The Children of Hamelin," "Inhabitants," "First Day of School after Christmas," and "When," in *Alabama Literary Review*; "Premises," in *Think*; "Halfser Astray," in *Able Muse*; and "At Middle Age," in *Presence*.

The author wishes to offer his deepest thanks to the editors of *Dappled Things*, Bernardo Aparicio and Katy Carl in particular, who enthusiastically agreed to support the composition and publication of "Quarantine Notebook" and made it possible for others to read the poem even as the events it describes were still taking place. This is in some ways their book; it would certainly not be without them. The author further wishes to thank Catharine Savage Brosman, Dana Gioia, A. M. Juster, Bill Thompson, and Ryan Wilson for their help in revising these poems.

About the Author

James Matthew Wilson has published nine previous books, including *The Hanging God* (Angelico, 2018) and *Some Permanent Things*, Second Edition, Revised and Expanded (Wiseblood, 2018). He is the recipient of the 2017 Hiett Prize from the Dallas Institute of Humanities and Culture; his poem "On a Palm" appeared in *Best American Poetry* 2018; and his work as a poet, critic, and scholar has been awarded various distinctions by the Conference on Christianity and Literature, the Catholic Press Association, *America* magazine, and *Dappled Things* magazine. Wilson serves as poetry editor of *Modern Age* magazine, the series editor of Colosseum Books, of the Franciscan University of Steubenville Press, and as the Director of the Colosseum Summer Institute. He is associate professor of Humanities and Augustinian Traditions at Villanova University, and Poet-in-Residence of the Benedict XVI Institute.

CPSIA information can be obtained
at www.ICGtesting.com
Printed in the USA
JSHW021928130123
36244JS00003B/140

9 781621 386322